Learning to read. Reading to learn!

LEVEL ONE Sounding It Out Preschool–Kindergarten
For kids who know their alphabet and are starting to sound out words.

learning sight words • beginning reading • sounding out words

LEVEL TWO Reading with Help Preschool–Grade 1
For kids who know sight words and are learning to sound out new words.

expanding vocabulary • building confidence • sounding out bigger words

LEVEL THREE Independent Reading Grades 1–3
For kids who are beginning to read on their own.

introducing paragraphs • challenging vocabulary • reading for comprehension

LEVEL FOUR Chapters Grades 2–4
For confident readers who enjoy a mixture of images and story.

reading for learning • ～～～～～～～～～ • feeding curiosity

Ripley Readers Designed to ～～～～～～～～～～ and confidence at any level, this program offers a variety of fun, entertaining, and unbelievable topics to interest even the most reluctant readers. With stories and information that will spark their curiosity, each book will motivate them to start and keep reading.

Vice President, Licensing & Publishing   Amanda Joiner
Editorial Manager   Carrie Bolin

Editor   Jessica Firpi
Writer   Korynn Wible-Freels
Designer   Scott Swanson
Reprographics   Bob Prohaska
Production Design   Luis Fuentes

Published by Ripley Publishing 2021

10 9 8 7 6 5 4 3 2 1

Copyright © 2021 Ripley Publishing

ISBN: 978-1-60991-405-9

For more information regarding permission, contact:
VP Licensing & Publishing
Ripley Entertainment Inc.
7576 Kingspointe Parkway, Suite 188
Orlando, Florida 32819

Email: publishing@ripleys.com
www.ripleys.com/books
Manufactured in China in May 2020.

First Printing

Library of Congress Control Number: 2020937132

PUBLISHER'S NOTE
While every effort has been made to verify the accuracy of the entries in this book, the Publisher cannot be held responsible for any errors contained in the work. They would be glad to receive any information from readers.

PHOTO CREDITS

Cover © Jeff Grabert/Shutterstock **3** © Jeff Grabert/Shutterstock **4-5** Colin Carter Photography via Getty Images **6-7** © Ondrej Prosicky/Shutterstock **8-9** © LesPalenik/Shutterstock **10-11** © RoSy76/Shutterstock **12-13** Gavin Bickerton-Jones via Getty Images **14-15** © JayPierstorff/Shutterstock **16-17** Tze-hsin Woo via Getty Images **18-19** © FJAH/Shutterstock **20-21** Thomas Pollin via Getty Images **22-23** © Milan Zygmunt/Shutterstock **24-25** © Maksimilian/Shutterstock **26-27** Mark Newman via Getty Images **28-29** By Milan Zygmunt **30-31** Natthawat via Getty Images **Master Graphics** Created by Scott Swanson

All other photos are from Ripley Entertainment Inc. Every attempt has been made to acknowledge correctly and contact copyright holders and we apologize in advance for any unintentional errors or omissions, which will be corrected in future editions.

Ripley Readers

Raging Raptors!

All true and unbelievable!

MARTIN COUNTY LIBRARY

RIPLEY
PUBLISHING

a Jim Pattison Company

Look up in the sky!

Can you see the raptor?

A raptor is a bird that
hunts for its food.

Another name for a raptor is a bird of prey.

They have round beaks and sharp claws to catch their food.

Did you know there are more than 500 kinds of raptors?

You can find them all over the world, even in your own backyard!

Look! The elf owl lives in a cactus!

It is as tall as a soda can.

All raptors eat meat.

They like fish, mice, rabbits, snakes, and other birds.

Some can take down big animals, like a deer!

Most birds of prey like
to hunt alone.

Only the Harris's hawk will hunt in groups of three or more.

Raptors have to be fast
to catch their food.

This falcon can fly 200 miles an hour!

Owls go hunting at night.

Their wings do not make
any sound when they fly!

A condor is the biggest bird of prey.

Wow! Look at the wings on that one!

Raptors can be little, too.

This bird of prey is only one foot long!

The name for a baby hawk or falcon is an eyas.

24

What a cute little bird!

Bald eagles can make really big nests!

This one is so deep you could stand in it!

A barn owl can have 11 babies!

How would you like that many brothers and sisters?

Did you know that people can train falcons to hunt for them?

What bird of prey do you think is the coolest?

All true and unbelievable!

Ready for More?

Ripley Readers feature unbelievable but true facts and stories!

**For more information about
Ripley's Believe It or Not!, go to www.ripleys.com**